Notes to Sing

poems by

Lee Harlin Bahan

Finishing Line Press
Georgetown, Kentucky

Notes to Sing

ACKNOWLEDGMENTS

"John Cougar Really Has Cousins Here" and "Almanac" first appeared in
Ploughshares.
"Reply, to a Friend in Boston" and "Jogging, City of the Elves" first appeared
in *Indiannual*.
"Midas" first appeared in *Plains Poetry Journal*.
"Rime of a Modern Mariner" first appeared in *Blue Unicorn*.
"December Field" first appeared in *Literally*.
"Midwinter Thaw, New England" first appeared in *Artful Dodge*.
"Canonicity" first appeared in *Painted Bride Quarterly*.
"Best Ladies' Room on U. S. 50" and "The Women and the Good News" first
appeared in *Cincinnati Poetry Review*.
"Drilling the Troops," "Last Bard in Wales," and "Hope" appeared originally
in *The Kenyon Review*, Spring 1991, Volume XIII, Number 2.
"At Gettysburg National Military Park" first appeared in *The North American
Review*.
"Manet's *Vase of White Lilacs and Roses*" first appeared in *The Mennonite*.

Editor: Christen Kincaid

Cover Art: Nick Walden

Author Photo: Pat Bahan

Cover Design: Elizabeth Maines

Printed in the USA on acid-free paper.
Order online: www.finishinglinepress.com
also available on amazon.com

Author inquiries and mail orders:
Finishing Line Press
P. O. Box 1626
Georgetown, Kentucky 40324
U. S. A.

Table of Contents

Vince Gotera—this, bud, is for you.

John Cougar Really Has Cousins Here

For years a sign near Randy Miser's yard
announced: MEDORA
            TOWN OF HARMONY
A bar of music showed beneath those words

the first notes of the scale ordered mi,
do, re. I've wondered driving in—to Mel's
for beer, past our shut-down factory—

what tune that railroad man was whistling while
he pounded ties. Who heard him, had the wit
to transpose song into a name for coal

bins and a water tank? Today we've got
a tavern, churches, one school K through 12
and a new sign. The old one was riddled with shot

one night—drunk boys likely, to amuse themselves.
Next day, before it disappeared, high winds
hammered that thing like a piano roll.

The town marshal, in thin-lipped silence,
I suppose, took it down for evidence.

Almanac

1. The sky is like the belly of a snake.

2. My mare shakes powdered sugar from her coat.

3. How much freeze and thaw can tulips take?

4. The river's out. We come and go by boat.

5. John Deeres upholster fields in corduroy.

6. Shoots flicker like heat lightning through the dust.

7. Wind sizzles in the cottonwoods. Fish fry.

8. At sunset wives fill paper sacks with husks.

9. Ripe walnuts thud like softballs on our lawn.

10. Rain drools across the fanlight, taps the roof.

11. Cats loot the kitchen trash for turkey bones.

12. Stalked redbirds track in snow brief epitaphs.

Reply, to a Friend in Boston

It isn't my days I want you to know
about, but waking at five, the bare
tree raking my window, hanging stars
in the glass. A little below

I can see town's bracelet of lights—also
cars shooting onto the highway. From here
they drive forty miles for bigger
paychecks, satellite dishes to go home to

after the lights have turned off and again
on. Being awake is like a space
between those lights. Today

no clouds encourage grass. I mean
nothing, only that leaves will make me miss
you, stranded light afloat on a black bay.

Remodeling Petrarch: Two Poems

Midas

Stay, love, review with me the day's parade
which, by exalting, seals our conquest.
Rain-silvered air becomes your looking glass.
Afterward, west light convinces blades

of grass they're emeralds. Surely it's God
in us that gilds and reads the sunset's page, sews
pearls on our native sackcloth. Shadows
cloister the hills, bead the switchback road.

For how could *failed* sight change an ancient oak
to onyx? Closed flowers beneath it pray
we'll walk there, touching them to gold again;

and the night, honeycombed with myth, is like
a minstrel trading fame for sanctuary,
eyes flickering with hearth-fire, our dark wine.

Rime of a Modern Mariner

I've been plugging along like this for years,
sighs in my wake, mateless on a toy tug
leaking fast as I bail, circling a moat I dug,
afraid of drowning on shores I gasp for.

So to hell with drying out. Pints of bitters
sweeten my disposition, cut the legs
out from under this devil, the one bugging
me to phone. What if a truck hits her?

Smoke fogs the bar until she's whores
the bathroom wall advertises. A bought fuck
would cost less than calling her. Drifting home

I salute whining German shepherds moored
to warehouse light poles near the dock,
marking fence, pissing on what they can't own.

Hangover

The party told the joke with the punch line
that no one remembers until the next
day when the bathroom door has to be fixed
because an old friend's new husband holds wine

even less well than her last. Squeaky blinds
blink. White light smiles sideways up each of six
snifters dodging miniature plastic
swords on the coffee table. As the pane

fogs, ashtrays emerge sparkling from water
almost too hot to bear. Order descends
more quietly than dust across armchairs

occupied by ghosts whose bodies elsewhere
breathe and speak. A bronze mum spends on clean chintz
petals irretrievable as laughter.

December Field

Snow-lathered stubble
invites the wind's razor. A
cedar bleeds redbirds.

Midwinter Thaw, New England

... their foot shall slide in due time.
—Deuteronomy 32:35

We're called inside by sacred Morse — a bell
pulled "Seven long," my host remarks, "three short."
The pews are Pilgrim hard. I guess the tolling

represents the week it took Our Lord
to create Earth and rest. I can't see why
the Trinity's rung fast — unless it's sort

of like the Catholics whose fingers fly
when making the cross. Pouring from a loft
in back of us, Bach preludes crystallize,

raise unseen scaffolding that shores the roof
reliably as Atlas. Antique panes
distort squirrels outside. Their leaps through leafless

trees graph random angles — as we drown
with hymns the frying sound of freezing rain.

Canonicity

If Eve had an alphabet besides bone,
weren't obliged to use a rat's rib to stitch
waterbags, flint to carve her husband's breech
clouts, or save scrap for catching blood each moon
she isn't pregnant, we'd have more to go on.

Her story disappeared with the cook-smoke.
Cain's dog whines and scratches at the mat, vacant
now for weeks, where her son slept. She suns
it every day, picking off nits, as if

he will come home. The river was a four
day walk and the reeds cut her fingers. *Waste
nothing*, evolution's answer to the curse,
burns her up. She would like to laugh
as Adam digs with a charred stick lines in dust.

Best Ladies' Room on U. S. 50

Versailles (verSAYLZ), town, SE IN, W of Cincinnati, OH
Plus ça change, plus c'est la même chose.

I'm sitting on a toilet in Versailles,
amazed a public restroom can be clean.
Most service station johns aren't mopped and leak
so dirty water soaks your tennis shoes
but keep—with blow-by-blow accounts of who-
does-what-how-often scribbled on the walls—

your mind off wet feet. These could be the walls
a nun lives in. Suppose the name *Versailles*
were said correctly—not by locals who
insist the other word that means "to clean"
is *warsh*—I'd be in France when wooden shoes
chafed novices toward sainthood, pouring leek

soup in an earthen bowl, checking for leaks
that might stain Reverend Mother's habit. Walls
marbleized with gilt recede as I shoo
flies—aswarm in summer at Versailles—
off simple food I carry, must keep clean
until it reaches Reverend Mother who

is here by God's command to save the Queen who
otherwise will land in Hell. Rose-smell leaks
from the royal chamber where, unclean
beneath the silk she's sewed in, mirrored walls
repeating her, the mistress of Versailles
sits eating chocolates and cashews.

I blush, embarrassed by my clunking shoes
and try to be like Reverend Mother who
sips soup, untempted to try on for size
those jeweled slippers that *pieds angeliques*
would fear to tread in. "Jericho's proud walls
collapsed," the R. M. warns while wiping clean

her lips, "as these will if you do not cleanse
this palace of its decadence. Eschew,
my daughter, worldly goods lest Mammon wall
you off from Heaven." In reply, the Queen, whose
skin is milk, chokes back a chuckle leaking
from her throat. "Our soul is not for sale,

our conscience, clean. The King hates golden shoes.
He leaked on his once, charmed by *La Joconde* who
watched, smiling from the wall here at Versailles."

Drilling the Troops

> *General Steuben remarked disgustedly that bayonets*
> *were chiefly used as skewers to broil meat.*
>> —*John B. B. Trussell, Jr.,* Epic on the Schuylkill

" … in Himmel. Ass mit bayonet I catch
roast meat again, I take it, cut der gott-
damn wienerwurst from him und feed to Brits
for fucking tea! Am funny son-of-bitch,

"eh, Hamilton? You laugh like Hell if reached
Burgoyne to Albany und burned estate
of liebchen's rich papa. Fight duel? Shit.
You douche-slime of a syphilitic crotch!
I lick you both hands tied behind. You fart
from mouth. Butt has more sense. Keep up this stink
und get new asshole chewed by Washington.

"Where was I? Ah—aim bayonet at heart
of charging horse und not to run, not blink.
No bastard will have balls to ride you down."

In the Vicinity of Valley Forge to Get Trout, 1787

Lately the State House had begun to stink. Good
then, to leave the flies of Philadelphia,
penny journals abuzz with scuttlebutt—*would
the General be king?*—speeches that snuff
couldn't sweeten after all night sessions
fueled by onion sandwiches & Madeira
in Publick Houses, strong opinion
stewing beneath French velvet, local wool—*an odor,*
the future President thinks, *like wet sheep.*
He motions Gouverneur Morris ahead,
says more gaily than he feels, "I'll not keep
you waiting. Don't catch all the fish," then rides
toward a sprouting field which, ten years ago,
grew empty bellies, rag-wrapped feet & snow.

At Gettysburg National Military Park

Unsure where to sign his mural-in-the-round,
Philippoteaux painted himself into the Cyclorama.

We climb a spiral ramp to stand inside
a half-wall circling a floor that I'm
afraid will lurch, then centrifuge like rides
at traveling carnivals, and drop. "How grim
the final dawn at Gettysburg," our park
guide drones while turning on a switch that shows
us how it would have felt to be *here*, marked
by spotlight, with 50,000 heroes
expiring at our feet. It's like The Bomb,
a hole in my imagination paints
can't fill. Untouched by what he's made, the artist
lounges against a tree. He, too, is lost
as "The Battle Hymn" drums us from the dimming room.
Outside, sun-striped cannon "ooh" in silence.

Last Bard in Wales

*a painting in the "William Wordsworth and the Age of
English Romanticism" exhibit, recollected à la Keats*

Now what I want to know is how this old
man with hair in his eyes and white samite
whipping around him managed x-number feet
above sea level if a goat couldn't've held
out because loose boulders would've rolled
at first hoof-strike and carrying a great
gold harp like Boston Pops or heaven not
a few catgut strings across a turtle shell.

Two pinnacles down the tyrant's mastiffs
strain at leashes keeping the throat safe
that suddenly might sing to them growling
the radiant bozo hasn't the decency to fear
a world infrequently here enough or we're
apart from it but in any case not for long.

Jogging, City of the Elves

Judging from the dirt and weedy parlors,
I'd say they left in 1904.

Maybe they had a party in the woods
and are still passed out. Maybe they signed on

with the Tooth Fairy—stacking bicuspids
here, molars there—saw television

coming and skedaddled. Indulgent
as the soft elastic in my shorts, their absence

amplifies a quail's call, begs a story
explaining why Gabriel would trade

his trumpet for one look at what I've been
flying over like a death angel. Beside the road

white, dime-sized cousins of the morning glory
at daybreak play mute gramophones.

Loony

Water drips on my forehead as I squirm
in my sleeping bag, due to a violent
christening slowed by the rain fly of our tent,
an irregular drip that will not harm
me really, but does bring the funny farm
to mind. I need to pee. Since I first imagined
bears tearing me like a Polish sausage
charred by lightning, I've needed to. Determined
not to go in the rain or wet my drawers,
I cross my legs, squeeze, try to doze. Stifling
urgency, I can hear beyond the muffling
waves. Loons call across the lake. Their whiffling
announces day and downpour turned to showers.
It is the sanest sound I've heard in hours.

The Women and the Good News

My husband waits till flood water warms
enough for carp to spawn, then calls his friend.
They take bows rigged with reels of string, arrows,
and paddle our canoe into the fields.

I drove my daughter to the church egg hunt
this morning. A boy screamed and waved his arms,
all but flung himself onto the gravel
so I'd not pull in. The sixth grade had set

eggs on the lot, figuring that little
kids would think the eggs were rocks. After service
last night, the stars were unmistakably

dust-like, kinder, farther away. We joked
about smelling hog farms south of us again,
swapped tips for egg salad, golden croquettes.

Hope

. . . is the thing with feathers
—Dickinson

Too much torque on a wing, and the branches
of the box elder, honeysuckle vines,
disappear. Each smack, when panic bounces
the bird off concrete blocks, ups its chances
of next time sailing back through a broken
window that my husband never fixes,
although I've asked him to time and again.
He finds them on the smokehouse floor, senseless.

I was in the bedroom, trying to mate
dark socks, when he offered me the redbird
like a wrong-shaped valentine. With it lying
left side down on his palm, still breathing
but staring elsewhere, I couldn't avoid,
in that black, the eye's minute point of light.

Manet's *Vase of White Lilacs and Roses*

Because Manet was dying, sunlight stamped
BEATIFIED across a pale pink rose,
the first of three that nail five lilac sprays,
more like Shiva's arms than Christ's, to a ground

so dark brown it's almost black. The glass
allows this darkness to invade the vase,
which, stained teak, describes a post that light
reflected by submerged foliage has carved.

The shadow cast by this arrangement falls
across a blue-veined marble table top
and briefly to the right. A window was
above, behind, and left of the artist's chair.

Dabs of paint on canvas prove and don't
what can't be argued. The vase and flowers form
a cross. If there's no window in this picture,
then neither is Manet, nor are you.

You're where the light is. Rising from the froth
of lilacs, one long stem with leaves insists
a bud exists although the canvas stops.

Thanks and Notes

This chapbook wouldn't exist without encouragement and criticism from Monica Barron, Daniel Bourne, Patrick Daily, Jeff Gundy, Marilyn Hacker, Andrew Hudgins, Mark Jarman, William Matthews *(in pace requiescat)*, Henry Taylor, and the gang at the Writers' Center of Indiana. I blow kisses to my husband Pat, editors who printed earlier versions of poems in this manuscript, and the denizens of the Eratosphere, whoever you really are.

"Midas" resulted when my imagination collided with Petrarch's *Rerum vulgarium fragmenta* 192.

Petrarch's *Rerum vulgarium fragmenta* 118 inspired "Rime of a Modern Mariner."

"Midwinter Thaw, New England" was drafted during a residency at Dorset Colony House, Dorset, Vermont.

Lee Harlin Bahan earned an A. A. degree at Santa Fe Community College, Gainesville, FL, and both a B. S., Ed. and M. F. A. in Poetry at Indiana University-Bloomington. For six years she taught an undergraduate creative writing course offered through I. U.'s Division of Continuing Studies, and did a sabbatical fill-in at DePauw University, Greencastle, IN, teaching a freshman poetry-as-literature course. She also has been an Artist in Education for the Indiana Arts Commission and substituted on a regular basis in the Medora Community Schools, Medora, IN.

Lee's first chapbook, *Migration Solo,* won the first Indiana Poetry Chapbook Contest and was published by the Writers' Center Press of Indianapolis. She received several Cummins Engine Foundation Fellowships, given to enable English teachers to attend the I. U. Writers' Conference. "Rime of a Modern Mariner," collected for the first time in *Notes to Sing,* was included in the manuscript for which Lee won the Nancy Armitage Award at the Sandhills Writers' Conference, Augusta, GA, 1987.

Along the way, the author has edited *Artful Dodge* and the Whoosier Network's *Gallifreyan Gazette,* as well as the newsletters of her local Habitat for Humanity chapter and her church. After receiving grant support from Driftwood Area Arts Council of Columbus, IN, to study Italian, Lee enjoyed a month-long residency at Mary Anderson Center for the Arts, Mt. St. Francis, IN, pursuing her goal of translating Petrarch's sonnets. Lee read from *A Year of Mourning,* her new, book-length group of Petrarch translations, at the University of Northern Iowa's *North American Review* Bicentennial Conference.